Second Voyage to Canada [Excerpts]

Jacques Cartier at Hochelaga

Our History in Pictures

Text adapted and presented by Françoise Ligier

Translated by Jane Macaulay

Smith, Bonappétit & Son

Montréal, Toronto

© 2008 Smith, Bonappétit & Son, Montréal (Canada),
and Françoise Ligier (text).

Legal Deposit: 3rd quarter 2008
Bibliothèque et Archives nationales du Québec
Library and Archives Canada

The publisher wishes to acknowledge the support of the
Canada Council for the Arts for this publishing program.
We are also thankful to the SODEC.

The translation of this book was made possible through
the financial support of the Canada Council for the
Arts and Heritage Canada through the Book Publishing
Industry Development Program.

Government of Quebec—Tax credit for book publishing—
Administered by SODEC.

Special thanks go to François-Marc Gagnon, scholar
and director of the Gail and Stephen A. Jarislowsky
Institute for Studies in Canadian Art, for his works
and the idea for this book.

Jacques Cartier at Hochelaga
Editor: Catherine Germain
Copy Editor: Marie Lauzon
Proof reader: Angèle Trudeau

Distributor for Canada: University of Toronto Press
**Bibliothèque et Archives nationales du Québec and
Library and Archives Canada cataloguing in publication**

Ligier, Françoise, 1937-

Jacques Cartier at Hochelaga: second voyage to Canada:
excerpts

(Our history in pictures)
Translation of: Jacques Cartier à Hochelaga.
For children.

ISBN: 978-1-897118-31-3

1. Cartier, Jacques, 1491-1557 - Travel - Juvenile literature.
2. America - Discovery and exploration - French - Juvenile
literature. 3. Montréal (Québec) - History - 16th century -
Juvenile literature. I. Cartier, Jacques, 1491-1557.
II. Title. III. Series.

FC301.C37A3 2007b   j971.01'13   C2007-942199-7

Printed in Canada by Transcontinental Métrolitho

L'insertion des M.rs compaignons mariniers et pilotes s'ensuyent

Jacques Cartier cap.ne)
(Thomas Fourmont M.re de la nef)

(Guill.e Lebreton Bastille cap.ne
et pilote du Gallon)

(Jacq Maingar M.re du Gallon)
(Marc Jalobert cap.t et pilote) (2))
du Courlieu)

(Guill.e Le Mane m.re du Courlieu)

(Laurent Boulain)

(Estienne Nouel)

(Pierre Esmery dict Talbot)

(Michel Herué)

(Estienne Rimeuel ou plus
Reumeve)
(Michel Audrepore)

(Bertrand Sambosce
ou Sambose)

(Richard Lebay)

(Lucas pere S.t Paucampe
ou Lucas Jacq S.t Pammye)

(1) Liste revue avec soin sur le Fac-simile, par C H Laverdière p.tre Bibliothecaire de l'Univ de Laval, 22 Novemb 1859. Dans l'original elle est divisee seulement en deux colonnes
(2) C'est le premier nom de la Petite Hermine.

For those who have come from afar
For those who have welcomed them
F.L.

In 1534, the French navigator Jacques Cartier arrived in Newfoundland for the first time. He had been sent by the King of France, François 1er, on a mission to find a new route to China and India, in search of spices and silk. Secretly, Cartier also hoped to discover "great quantities of gold and many rich things," as the Spanish conquistadors had done in South America.

Before this date, the coasts of North America had been regularly visited by Breton, Basque and Norman mariners, who came to fish cod or hunt whales. But once this seasonal activity was over, the seamen returned to their home ports, having little interest in learning more about the people who inhabited this unknown land.

Jacques Cartier, however, came to observe, take notes, draw maps and

meet the Native population, learning much from their store of knowledge. He made three trips to what is now Canada. Although Cartier's own maps seem to have disappeared, his

observations and the names he gave places are found on most of the maps made in this period. The accounts of his three voyages have been preserved.

Map: Pierre Descelliers (1546). This large map (almost four metres wide) is upside down to our eyes, since the north is at the bottom. It enabled King François 1er of France to understand Jacques Cartier's explorations and, in a way, served to illustrate his accounts.

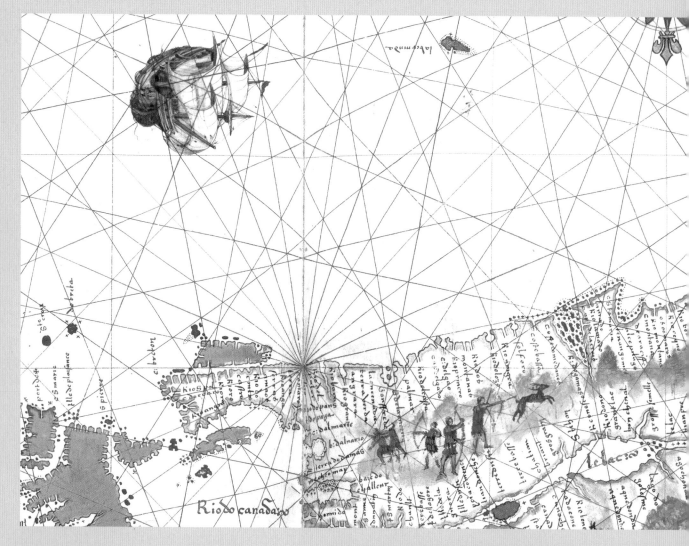

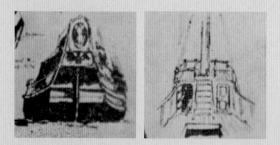

The following passages are taken from a chapter in *Brief Recit* by Jacques Cartier, published in Paris in 1545.

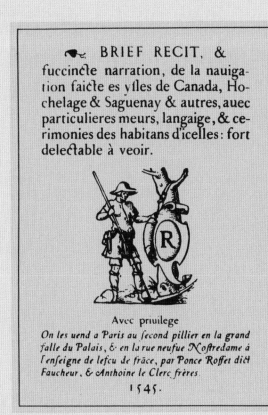

The year was 1535

Aboard three ships, Jacques Cartier and his men sailed inland along the St. Lawrence River. They stopped at Stadacona, the town that would later become the city of Québec, then took the smallest of their ships, the *Émerillon*, and continued upstream towards Hochelaga (now known as Montréal), hoping to discover a passage to the Orient.

But when they reached Lake Saint-Pierre, the vessel could go no further. The river, dotted with numerous islands, was no longer deep enough. The ship was too heavy and hard to steer in these waters. Leaving a few men on board, Cartier and the rest of the crew continued on their way in rowboats. It is here that our story begins...

F.L.

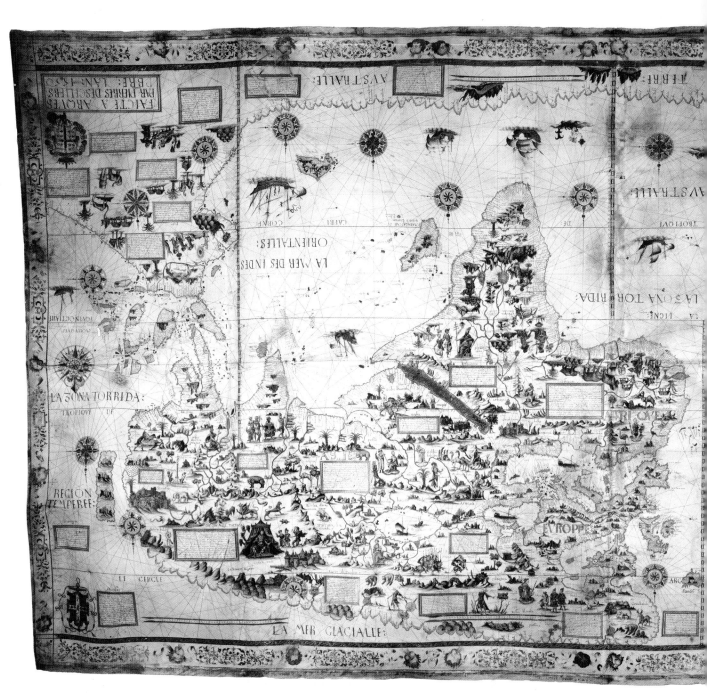

Nostre cappitaine, voyant qu'il n'estoit possible de pouvoir, pour lors, passer ledict gallion, fist avictailler et acoustrer les barques, et mectre victuailles pour le plus de temps qu'il fut possible…

Map: Pierre Descelliers (1550).

Seeing that our galleon could not pass, the captain had the rowboats prepared. He ordered that they should be loaded with as many provisions as possible, for the trip might well be long. Then he went aboard and departed, accompanied by a few gentlemen and sailors.

We navigated in pleasant weather for about forty-five leagues and arrived at Hochelaga on the second day of October.

The next day, at daybreak, the captain put on his finest clothes ★ and ordered us to prepare ourselves with care before going to see the town, its houses and inhabitants, and the nearby mountain.

We followed a well-made road across rich, fertile fields. We admired oak trees, as grand as any in France, and the ground beneath them was covered with acorns.

Map: Vallard Atlas (ca. 1547).

*Besides their way to dress, it is interesting to note the presence of women amongst the group of Frenchmen. As there were no women in Jacques Cartier's second trip, we know that we have here an illustration of his third trip. Jacques Cartier himself might be the one pointing towards the west.

Le landemain, au plus matin, le cappitaine se acoustra, et fict mectre ses gens en ordre, pour aller veoyr la ville et demourance dudict peuple, et vne montaigne, qui est jacente à ladicte ville …

When we had walked about a league and a half, we met a leader of the town of Hochelaga ★, accompanied by several people. He signalled to us that we should take a rest beside a bonfire they had made. We accepted this invitation. Our captain offered him two axes, two knives and two crucifixes, and the leader thanked us for these gifts.

Nous aians marché environ lieue et demye, trouvasmes sus le chemin l'vn des principaulx seigneurs de ladicte ville de Hochelaga, avecq plusieurs personnes, lequel …

* This town was located near a lake where many beavers lived, and the name Hochelaga came from the Iroquoian word for "Beaver Lake." However, the exact position of this site has never been identified with certainty. Historians think that the settlement had a population of about two thousand inhabitants. At the time, the name Hochelaga referred to the river that is now called the St. Lawrence, as well as the town later known as Montréal and the "province" or "kingdom" in which it lay.

* This cereal was what we call corn (in British English, all cereals in general are referred to as "corn"). The comparison with Brazilian millet suggests that Jacques Cartier had previously visited that country. Note that the setting appears European, for the illustrators were Europeans who had never seen North America.

We then continued on our way, walking among vast fields that were full of the cereal they grow here instead of wheat ★. The seeds of this plant are as big as a pea, or even bigger, and the people here use them as millet is used in Brazil, or wheat in France. The town of Hochelaga is situated in the midst of this fertile countryside, near a mountain, which we named Mount Royal.

Ce faict, marchames plus oultre, et envyron demye lieu de là, commençasmes à trouver les terres labourées et belles, grandes champaignes, plaines de bledz de leur terre...

The town of Hochelaga is circular in shape ★. It is surrounded by a stockade consisting of three rows of wooden stakes laced together in a complex manner. At several points, there are galleries of sorts and ladders for guards to keep watch. The town is entered by a single gate that can be firmly closed.

The interior of the town is made up of some fifty houses measuring fifty paces or more in length and twelve or fifteen paces in width. The houses are all made of wood and covered with broad strips of bark, solidly sewn together.

★ The perfect symmetry of this plan probably did not correspond to reality. The drawing is yet another example of European illustrators using their imagination.

Ladicte ville est toute ronde, et cloze de boys, à troys rancqs, en façon d'vne piramyde, croizée par le hault, ayant la rangée du parmy en façon de ligne perpendicullaire…

Each house has several rooms. In the middle there is a large room with a mud floor where the inhabitants make their fire and live as a group. Every house also has rooms to which each family can retire. Above the living area there is a garret where they store the grain they use to make their bread, which they call *carraconny*.

With this grain, as well as beans and peas, which they have in sufficient quantity, the inhabitants of this village make many soups. They also have large cucumbers and other fruit.

In their houses, there are big wooden recipients like barrels. These are used to store fish that is dried and smoked during the summer, especially eel.

Et par dedans icelles y a plusieurs aistres et chambres; et au meilleu d'icelles maisons, y a vne grande salle par terre, où ilz font leur feu, et vivent en communauté...

They sleep on pieces of bark spread on the ground, with blankets made with the pelts of otters, beavers, martins, foxes, raccoons, stags, deer and other wild animals. These pelts are also used for making clothing, even though the great majority of these people are practically naked.

From the river, they take a white shell called *esnoguy*, with which they make a kind of necklace. In their eyes, it is the most precious thing in the world, since they use it as we do silver and gold.

These people devote themselves to farming and fishing. They are thus not a nomadic people, as the people of Canada and Saguenay ★.

★ The region was inhabited by three Iroquoian communities, which Cartier referred to as "kingdoms":

1. The kingdom of Canada, extending from about Île-aux-Coudres in the east to Achelacy (now Portneuf) in the west. Stadacona (Québec) was the most important town.
2. The kingdom of Hochelaga, centred around the town of Hochelaga, which later became Montréal.
3. The kingdom of Saguenay, a mysterious place, full of precious metals and difficult to reach.

Et couchent sus escorces de boys, estandues sus la terre, avecq meschantes couvertures de peaulx de bestes sauvaiges de quoy font leur vestemens et couverture . . .

★ Note in the illustration the child who appears to be playing "horsey." Since the horse was unknown in this part of North America, the image may be another instance of European illustrators relying on their own culture and imagination.

Ainsi comme fumes arrivez auprès d'icelle ville, se randirent audavant de nous grand numbre des habitants d'icelle, lesquelz, à leur façon de faire, nous firent bon raqueil...

When we arrived near the town, a
large number of its inhabitants came
to us and gave us a warm welcome,
in their manner.

The women and young girls, some of
them with children in their arms ★,
gathered together. Then they came and
rubbed our faces, arms and other parts
of the body, weeping with joy to see us.

They offered us food and made us
understand that they wished us
to touch their children.

· PORC · EPIC · SAVAGE ·

Then the King and lord of the land, whom they call the *Agouhanna*, arrived. He was carried by nine or ten men and was seated on a large stag pelt. This man, who appeared to be ill, was about fifty years old. Apart from a red band of hedgehog ★ quills that he wore as a crown, he was dressed like the others.

When he had made a sign of greeting to the captain and his men, he showed the captain his arms and legs, indicating that he wished him to touch them, as if he was asking to be healed and made healthy again. The captain rubbed his arms and legs. The *Agouhanna* then lifted off his crown and gave it to the captain. Then he had all the sick people come.

Seeing the poor souls, the captain read passages from the Gospel ★★ to all these attentive, silent people, who imitated our every gesture.

*Après lesquelles choses ainsi faictes, fut apporté,
par neuf ou dix hommes, le Roy et seigneur du pays,
qu'ilz appellent en leur langue « agouhanna »,
lequel estoit assiz sus vne grande peau de serf…*

* The "hedgehog" to which Jacques Cartier referred was actually a porcupine, an animal that was unknown in Europe.

** In a letter addressed to the "Very Christian King François the first" before this second expedition, Jacques Cartier spoke of his ambition to spread the "very holy Christian faith" wherever his travels took him. On his first trip in 1534, Cartier had raised a large cross near Gaspé. When the Iroquoians of Stadacona and their chief Donnacona, who were fishing along the shore, showed their displeasure, Cartier had explained that it was simply a reference point.

After that, the captain divided the men, women and children into three groups. To the men he gave hatchets and knives; to the women he presented little crosses and other small articles; and then he distributed rings and religious medals to the children.

This having been done, the captain ordered that trumpets and other musical instruments be sounded.

Seeing that we were about to leave, the women brought us food: fish, soup, beans, bread and other things. But since this food lacked salt, it was not to our taste and we thanked them, saying that we were not hungry.

Après laquelle, fist ledict cappitaine ranger tous les hommes d'vn cousté, les femmes d'vn aultre et les enfants d'aultre, et donna aux principaulx des hachotz, es aultres des couteaulx...

MONTE REAL.

* The mountains to the north of the St. Lawrence were the Laurentians, while those to the south were the Appalachians.

** According to some, the boats were left at the Sault au Récollet Rapids, while others think they were left at the Lachine Rapids.

*** The three mountains are Mount Saint-Bruno, Mount Saint-Hilaire and Mount Saint-Grégoire.

After we had left the town, we were led to the top of the mountain which we named Mount Royal. From there, we had a view that showed mountains both to the north and to the south *, and between them a good plain, suitable for farming, on either side of the river. In one direction, there was the place where we had left our boats **, where rapids had made it impossible for us to continue, and in the other direction, the river was broad and spacious, passing by three beautiful round mountains ***.

Après que nous fumes sortis de ladicte ville, fumes conduictz par plusieurs hommes et femmes d'icelle sur la montaigne... par nous nommée Mont Royal, distant dudict lieu d'vn cart de lieue...

Après lesquelles choses ainsi venues et entendues, nous retirasmes à noz barques qui ne fut sans avoir conduicte de grand numbre dudict peuple, dont partie d'eulx, quant veoyoient nos gens laz…

After that, preceded by a great number of men and women, we set off for the place where we had left our boats. Some of the men, seeing that our people were tired, lifted them on their backs and carried them as horses would.

We left these people with regret. Many of them followed us down the river as far as they could.

We arrived at the *Émerillon* on the fourth day of October and then prepared to return to the province of Canada, where our ships, the *Grande Hermine* and *Petite Hermine*, had stayed.

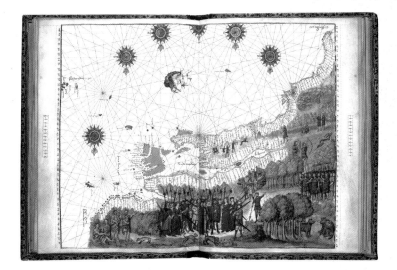

Illustration Credits